W9-BWT-435

CAN YOU IMAGINE?

Being a

MANATEE

By
Mary Molly
Shea

Gareth Stevens
Publishing

Please visit our website, www.garethstevens.com. For a free color catalog of all our high-quality books, call toll free 1-800-542-2595 or fax 1-877-542-2596.

Library of Congress Cataloging-in-Publication Data

Shea, Mary Molly.
Being a manatee / by Mary Molly Shea.
   p. cm. — (Can you imagine?)
Includes index.
ISBN 978-1-4824-3278-7 (pbk.)
ISBN 978-1-4824-3279-4 (6-pack)
ISBN 978-1-4824-0127-1 (library binding)
1. Manatees — Juvenile literature. I. Shea, Mary Molly. II. Title.
QL737.S63 S22 2014
599.55—dc23

First Edition

Published in 2014 by
Gareth Stevens Publishing
111 East 14th Street, Suite 349
New York, NY 10003

Copyright © 2014 Gareth Stevens Publishing

Designer: Katelyn E. Reynolds
Editor: Therese Shea

Photo credits: Cover, p. 1 A Cotton Photo/Shutterstock.com; cover, pp. 1–32 (background texture) AnnabelleaDesigns/Shutterstock.com; p. 5 Achimdiver/Shutterstock.com; pp. 7, 21 Franco Banfi/WaterFrame/Getty Images; p. 9 Jupiterimages/Photos.com/Thinkstock.com; p. 11 (West Indian manatee), 15 (inset), 17, 24 iStockphoto/Thinkstock.com; p. 11 (Amazonian manatee) Mark Bowler/Photo Researchers/Getty Images; p. 11 (West African manatee) pelican from Tokyo, Japan/Wikipedia.com; p. 13 Mark Conlin/Oxford Scientific/Getty Images; p. 15 (main) Alastair Pollock Photography/Flickr/Getty Images; p. 19 Brian J. Skerry/National Geographic/Getty Images; p. 22 Comstock/Thinkstock.com; p. 23 Mauricio Handler/National Geographic/Getty Images; p. 25 Dennis Macdonald/Photographer's Choice RF/Getty Images; p. 27 Jeff Foott/Discovery Channel Images/Getty Images; p. 28 Liquid Productions, LLC/Shutterstock.com; p. 29 romarti/Shutterstock.com.

Printed in the United States of America

CPSIA compliance information: Batch #CW14GS: For further information contact Gareth Stevens, New York, New York at 1-800-542-2595.

CONTENTS

Words in the glossary appear in **bold** type the first time they are used in the text.

JUST IMAGINE

Imagine swimming slowly through warm waters. You see some tasty-looking sea grass and stop for a bite to eat. Then, you rise to the water's surface so you can take a breath. You're hungry again and begin to look for some more delicious plants. You're about 10 feet (3 m) long and weigh 1,000 pounds (454 kg), so you really like to eat!

You're picturing the slow-moving life of the gentle **mammal** called the manatee. Read on to learn more about this large and lovable creature.

imagine that!

Manatees are related to elephants!

Manatees are large **marine** mammals. Their favorite activities are eating and resting!

BIG BODIES

Manatees are big and heavy. If you were an adult manatee, you could weigh as much as 3,000 pounds (1,362 kg) and measure 13 feet (4 m) long! Female manatees are usually a bit larger than males.

Manatees need power to push their huge bodies through water. They have a strong, flat tail called a paddle that can do this. They use their front **flippers** to change directions. In very shallow water, manatees may crawl with their front flippers.

imagine that!

Some kinds of manatees have fingernails on their flippers.

Most manatees are about 10 feet (3 m) long and weigh about 1,000 pounds (454 kg). Some are smaller, and some are larger.

TINY EARS AND EYES

If you were a manatee, you'd probably use your sense of hearing more than sight. Manatees may be big, but they have tiny ears and eyes. Each ear opening is a very small hole behind the eyes. Manatees can hear very well, though. Large ear bones and cheekbones under their skin pick up sounds in the water.

Manatee eyes are small as well. They probably see blue and green colors, and see just well enough to find food in the water.

imagine that!

Manatees make sounds when they're scared or angry. They chirp, whistle, and squeak.

ear

eye

After studying two manatees, scientists said the big marine mammals would be considered legally blind if they were people!

9

KINDS OF MANATEES

There are three **species** of manatees. All are a grayish color. Amazonian manatees are the smallest. They live in the Amazon River of South America. West African manatees live in the rivers and waterways along the western coast of Africa.

West Indian manatees live from the southern East Coast of the United States to Brazil. The Florida manatee is a kind of West Indian manatee. Which kind of manatee would you want to be?

imagine that!

Some people think dwarf manatees are a fourth species. Others think they're just a smaller kind of Amazonian manatee.

West Indian manatee

The Amazonian manatee lacks the fingernails on its flippers that the other two species have.

West African manatee

Amazonian manatee

11

WANTING WARMTH

If you were a manatee, you'd hate the winter. The Florida manatee doesn't like water cooler than 70°F (21°C). Since shallower waters are warmer, they like to live there. Florida manatees are rarely seen in waters more than 20 feet (6 m) deep.

Florida manatees may swim as far north as Virginia when the weather is warmer there. One manatee was even spotted near Cape Cod, Massachusetts! This is very unusual, though. By November, Florida manatees travel back south.

imagine that!

Female manatees are called cows. Male manatees are called bulls.

Manatees are drawn to warm waters around power plants, as this photo shows.

13

WHAT'S THAT GREEN STUFF?

The Amazonian manatee never goes into salt water. West Indian and West African manatees can live in both freshwater and salt water, but they need to drink freshwater. They also get water from the plants they eat.

Can you picture growing green stuff on your skin? You'd probably want to take a bath! Manatees are already in the water, and their skin is a great place for **algae** to grow. Manatees in salt water may have barnacles on them, too. Barnacles are small, shell-covered marine creatures.

imagine that!

Manatees were once land animals!

Algae like to grow on wet places with lots of sunlight, like a manatee's back!

barnacles

15

GOOD TRICK!

Manatees have to hold their breath underwater, just like you do. But if you were a manatee, you could hold your breath underwater up to 20 minutes! You'd usually come up every 3 or 4 minutes, though.

When manatees come up for a breath, they push their open **nostrils** above water. When they're underwater, they close up the nostrils.

Manatees sleep underwater for short periods at a time. They may surface to breathe while they're sleeping!

imagine that!

Some think mermaid tales came from sailors spotting manatees from a distance!

Munatees can stay underwater for longer periods when they're resting.

17

JUST SALAD, PLEASE

Can you imagine eating salad—and nothing else—for the rest of your life? If you were a Florida manatee, you'd be an herbivore (UHR-buh-vohr), which means you'd only eat plants. Eating grass might sound boring, but Florida manatees eat 60 different kinds! Other kinds of manatees sometimes eat clams and fish, but they're mostly plant eaters, too.

Manatees eat plants floating in the water, growing on the seafloor, or even hanging in branches over the water. They have **flexible** lips that allow them to grab plants easily.

imagine that!

Manatees have whiskers. Scientists know the whiskers feed information to their brain.

Sometimes manatees eat fish and bugs by accident while they're chowing down on plants.

CALVES

Manatees gather in groups when it's time to **mate**. If you were a manatee, you'd be born underwater! And you'd be a big baby—as long as 3.5 feet (1.1 m) and about 65 pounds (30 kg)! Manatee babies are called calves. Mother manatees give birth every 2 to 5 years to just one baby at a time.

Mothers push their baby to the surface to take its first breath. About an hour later, the manatee calf can swim by itself!

imagine that!

Scientists believe that manatees can live to be 60 years old.

A manatee calf sticks close to its mother and needs to drink her milk.

21

NO NEED FOR SPEED

If you were a manatee, you wouldn't have to worry about sharks, alligators, or other predators. Manatees don't have any enemies in nature! This might be why they're slow moving. They don't have to swim to escape anything.

Manatees also don't have to travel in groups for safety as schools of fish and pods of dolphins do. They're often alone or in pairs. You might see a group of manatees together if there's a lot of food in one area or a warm spot of water.

People shouldn't feed manatees. It's actually against the law! The food might harm them.

WATCH OUT!

As a manatee, your greatest enemy would be boats! Even if manatees wanted to move fast, it would be hard to move faster than a speedboat. Manatees in the way of a boat are often hurt or killed.

Boat **hulls** can run into manatees in shallow waters or coming up for air in deeper waters. Boat **propellers** can slice into a manatee's skin. Many manatees have cuts on their bodies showing where boats hit them. Scientists are worried that manatee populations won't bounce back unless something is done.

MANATEE ZONE
SLOW SPEED
MINIMUM WAKE

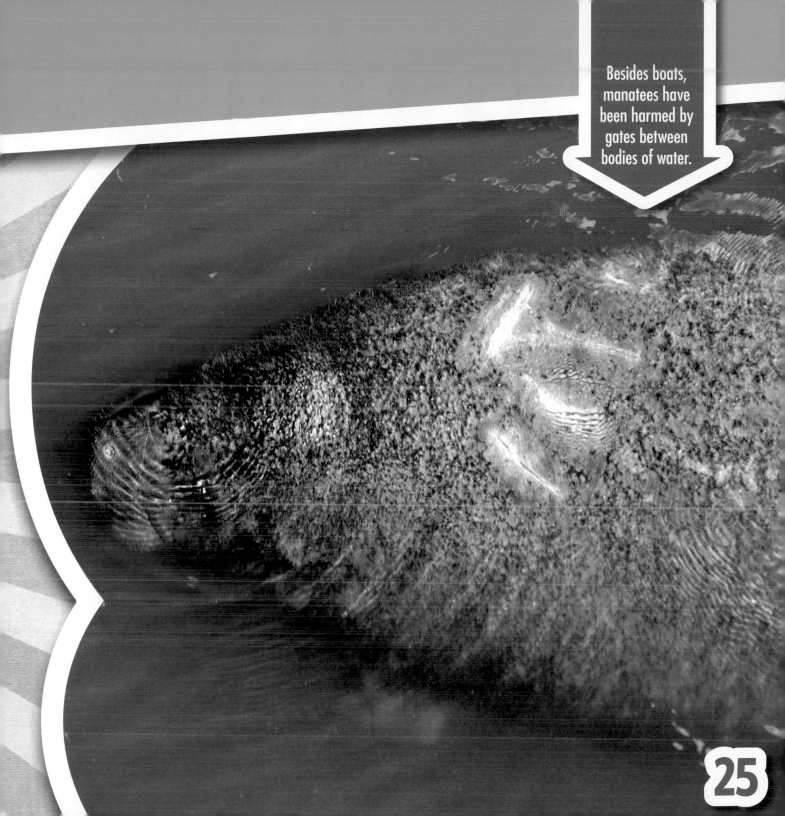

Besides boats, manatees have been harmed by gates between bodies of water.

25

RED TIDE

When certain kinds of algae grow too much, they can harm sea creatures. Scientists call them harmful algal blooms, and others call them red tides. These algae have been killing many Florida manatees. They grow on sea grasses that the manatees eat and act as a poison. Manatees may drown in just a few feet of water after eating the algae.

Some scientists are taking action to help sick manatees. They find and catch manatees and help them come up for air every few minutes until they can breathe by themselves.

imagine that!

Manatees can eat 100 pounds (45 kg) of plants a day, so it's hard to stop them from eating dangerous algae.

Red tide grows when water temperature and other conditions are just right. It turns the water reddish-brown.

27

ENDANGERED

Amazonian and West African manatee populations have been hard to count. They face another danger—people hunting for their meat. Sightings are becoming more rare.

There are about 3,200 Florida manatees left. They're **endangered**. Because a female manatee has just one baby every few years, it's hard for the population to grow quickly. People are trying to come up with solutions for boating accidents and harmful algal blooms. Manatees have no enemies except people, so it's up to us to save them!

mother and baby

Florida Manatee Deaths (2008–2013)

Manatees may not try to escape from boats because they don't connect the sights and sounds to danger.

Year	Deaths
2008	337
2009	429
2010	766
2011	453
2012	392
2013*	617

* as of June 2013

GLOSSARY

algae: plantlike living things that are found mostly in water

endangered: in danger of dying out

flexible: able to bend easily

flipper: a wide, flat "arm" used for swimming

hull: the body of a ship

mammal: a warm-blooded animal that has a backbone and hair, breathes air, and feeds milk to its young

marine: having to do with the sea

mate: to come together to make babies

nostril: an opening through which an animal breathes

propeller: paddle-like parts on a ship that spin in the water to move the ship forward

species: a group of plants or animals that are all of the same kind

FOR MORE INFORMATION

Books

Lourie, Peter. *The Manatee Scientists: Saving Vulnerable Species.* Boston, MA: Houghton Mifflin Books for Children, 2011.

Owen, Ruth. *Manatee Calves.* New York, NY: Bearport, 2013.

Skerry, Brian. *Face to Face with Manatees.* Washington, DC: National Geographic, 2010.

Websites

Florida Manatee
www.defenders.org/florida-manatee/basic-facts
Find out what people are doing to help manatees.

Manatee
animals.nationalgeographic.com/animals/mammals/manatee/
Read more about these gentle creatures.

INDEX